I dedicate this collection of my poetry to my family. My amazing 3 children Sean, Adrian, and Meagan. My astounding grandchildren; Josiah, Zayden, Angel, Rylan, A'Marrah, Shaielle, Ryan, Maliyah, Jayceon, and Sariah.
You All Are My Light!

There's a little lady in me that wants out

To turn on music and dance all about

Never being serious

Always curious

She only sees the good in all

No built up walls

For she still believes she can be a star

She never sees her scars

She's never been hit

In a corner she'll never sit

She wakes up with a smile on her face

No bad memories to erase

That little lady is now 52 year old

Battered, bruised and a heart of mold

Something about the first time you are struck
Your inner reasoning runs amuck
The shock
Was that a cinderblock
How could thee
Strike ME
I always said this was a never
I am way too clever
Never I
Now that's a lie
Now they carry my dignity in their hand
I feel this invisible quicksand
No one will believe me
Thou is thought of high morality
The replay will not stop
I can't call a cop
Im sure this was an accident
Did I provoke this event
I must be on my P's and Q's
I had no clues
Do I stay? Do I go?
Deep down I know
The right thing to do
Accidents like this are far and few
Leave now? Escape this pain?
Before it is my casket being lowered in the rain.

I I didn't see you
The door was open, so I walked through
I had stayed in this dark room waiting for years
So many battles, so many tears
I called your name, no I screamed out to you
How could you have left me, how could you
 I began to sulk in pity each day
I let my soul waste away
Filled with bitterness, I became empty
When I looked in the mirror there was a ghost looking
back at me
Dark circles under my eyes
No longer water in my cries
Words without a voice
I danced to music playing Satan's noise
Left on a bridge awakened by rocks in my teeth
I had no vision only sounds of strangers saying she cant
breathe
Your hand was over my heart
You leaned forward, telling me you carried me from the
start
It was Satan's room I had chosen to walk into and you
had been waiting patiently
Now is not your time, there still are great plans for me
I gasped and awoke with real tears
Gods love will keep me for the rest of my years

I raised my head from prayer

A familiar sight, no one was sitting here

3 empty chairs at my table

I keep reminiscing of my childhood fable

It's now became my own biography

When read out loud , I'm not that fond of me

Seeing my friends are now gone, I'm out of pleas

I thought we all were thick as thieves

Marriages, babies, divorces, deaths, we were so tight

We stayed on the phone all hours of the night

I don't even remember a goodbye or dismissal

One left in silence, one in anger, the last in belittle

Their chairs we filled for over twenty years

I must be drunk on my swallowed tears

Left Again

That's the name carved on the seat I sit in

Lets take our last breath together

Put an end to our fake forever

The roller coaster of our love

I pull you shove

I beg you to leave

When I really crave reciprocity

No ones touch makes me as high

I almost touch the sky

I want to feel your breath

Your my meth

Lets avoid the pain of goodbye

In each others vain we will die

I'm still in awe

Is that you I just saw

Its been so long

Time has done you wrong

I tried not to be rude and stare

The eyes looking back were so bare

Reality is very clear

It was my soul in the mirror

Monsters are not born they are created
Once full of joy, somewhere left devastated
It could have been just one word
Something they overheard
And then began the rejection seeds
Watered for years, filled with weeds
An emptiness
Only anger could guide the harness
Black sheep of the family
Suddenly he commits a tragedy
Oh how could he
Yet everyone could see
But those closest to his heart
He was scorned from an early start
Everyone looked the other way
Until today
Trying to comfort their guilt
Never adhering to their role in how he felt
Words can build or destroy
Careful how you stack them, you might build a devils toy

I was always told to look down , beneath the bar

Keeping my eyes on the ground, I never saw a single star

Red hair, green eyes, freckles all over me

I was as odd as odd could ever be

I'd click my dirty heels when no one was looking my way

Close my eyes, and beg God to take me far, far away

Please take me, I promise to be quiet and kind

I'll stay hidden, my being you'll never find

I begged daily until I believed God had moved on

At age 17 my self esteem was gone

I found love in the devils arms

Holiday memories of broken charms

Now 43 and still clicking my heels

Keeping my eyes lowered to window sills

there's really not a first place

A last place

there's just this space

A presence

if your real still

very still

you can feel

an omnipresence

oh so effervescent

inside ones own being

just from being

silently

still

in your own place

As a child I was not caressed

I was only sternly addressed

Nurturing was never on display

My smiles merely brought dismay

So I assumed I was unworthy

Unconditional love would never find me

Each morning I hated looking in the mirror

Until today, I saw Hope in her

Maybe love won't hurt so bad

Maybe love won't make me sad

I've just never felt it, not truly

Never unconditionally

I do have hope, is that enough

Love should not have to be so tough

No more hurt, lies and fears

I'm ready for those happy tears

I just prayed for you

For you do not know what you do

There is so much pain inside of you

May God make you brand new

Let go of the old that you knew

All the ones that hurt you

God will not forsake you

This is your day , love is meant for you too

Falling down does not make you a failure

Its really an exposure

To what you truly can endure

Oh it hurts for sure

Each time pain visits fewer

That's how one has found the greatest cures

Its the getting up where victory is measured

Put your hands down

Turn your thoughts around

Pause and pray

Make this be your best day

Hate is too hard to grow

Love is so much easier to sew

Your not the only one on pain

Be that one that dances in the rain

Smile through your tears

Joy will give your life many years

At the end of your days

What will your obituary say

At age 2, 5, 25, and 52

The words you labeled me were really reflections of you

I no longer fit in the box you've kept me in

That's your sin

I'm giving your mess back to you

I'll even pack it up pretty, make it all brand new

I now have one shot at this thing called life

Carrying around your opinion is too much strife

I yearned for your approval more than even air

That stamp never came, I'll ask God why if I get upstairs

Dear younger me

If you could see

Your amazing story

You'd stop the worry

Shed half as much tears

Realize all those inner fears

Were just that 1 inch inner voice

Always making unnecessary noise

But it made you humble

The Lord never let you fumble

If I'd knew then what I know now

I'd give grave a bow

Dear younger me

Just believe

THERE IS A RAW BEAUTY IN PAIN

ITS JUST YOU AND GOD

IT REVEALS YOUR TRUE CORE SELF

THAT IS THE MOST IMPORTANT PERSON

YOU WILL EVER MEET

So here I am

A new ma'am

Take me as I am

Flaws and all

Ten feet tall

Or so I think, right now

Give me your all, right now

For I deserve only the best

For the rest

Of my life

With your life

Lets do this test

The best

We can

My friend

I reach

You teach

One chance

Lets dance

I'm free

You no longer have a hold on me

You kept trying

I kept denying

For so long I only heard your voice

Telling me I had no choice

Telling me I was of no worth

That I should leave this earth

But now the rose inside of me

Has bloomed to see

My inner beauty

No mom, you I will never be

You mock me when I beg you to go

Please, please put an end to this circus show

Most people wakeup with delight

My eyes open with fright

Slowly listening for your breath

Wondering if you just finished a line of meth

Will this be your last day or mine

I'm done bargaining with father time

You're the only drug I've ever tried

Your label should read * love him and your soul will die *

The only way out I see is a permanent demise

Through these eyes

My vision

Has led me to this final decision

No longer my mind will you cottle

While I have my senses I must destroy this empty pill bottl

Yes you see my flaws because I show you

But that does not mean I am not as pretty as you

Yes I have revealed my insecurities to you

But don't think it makes me weak to you

I choose how I treat you

It is only my character that I will have to answer to

Binding me daily

Tricking me into saying

I'm not this I'll never be that

He'll never want me I'm to fat

My worst enemy

Trapped inside of me

My only company

Because of you I can't keep a friend

To shut you down I often plot your end

How amazing you can be for strangers

The MIND, when tormented; a tragic danger

I'M SCREAMING
BUT NO ONE LISTENS
YET WHEN SILENT
EVERYONE HAS QUESTIONS

IS LIFE JUST A GAME OF CHESS
A TEST OF MENTAL WARFARE
WHAT IS TRUE PEACE
DOES ONE PHYSICALLY ARRIVE THERE

My love for you was so real

Like that of an onion peel

With every layer; deeper love I would feel

Then I passed you with Jyl

My being was frozen still

That emotion began to reel

Revenge stayed on even keel

It became a minute by minute ordeal

My brokenness I could no longer conceal

Pre-meditated sounds so unreal

I am pleading for a lessor deal

Boy I have seen some Mess

And walked through it

It hangs with the best

It will have your emotions lit

Mess likes to plot and wait

You are fine, humming through your Wednesday

Sitting outside, watching your kids skate

Then bam, you over hear what your neighbors say

He s been cheating for a long time

And she's much prettier

You think your going to loose your mind

You knew all along there was another

But you just sit and hum

You smile, plotting your revenge Mess

He'll never know where this came from

Now time to go pick out your funeral dress

Today I mourn what we are not
I'll never understand how things got
Right here
This level of tears
How do I live without you
What will I do
Life can be so unkind
Can we rewind
Back to yesterday
When things were okay
When we said our vows
Not knowing how
To just Love
Only how to shove
Never listening to each other
Yet oh such magic lovers
Then distance settled in
Like next of kin
We felt more like sisters and brothers
We forgot how to talk to each other
And then the phone call came
My life will never been the same
A 6 pound baby boy
He should have been my joy
The joy you found in my sister
It's been 10 years now since you chose her

I'm curious

Do you believe half which you say

I'm curious

Do you ever just pause and pray

I'm curious

Why must you always play

I'm curious

What would you do if this were your last day

I'm curious

Why do you wrap yourself in such dismay

I'm curious

Why you could never meet me halfway

I'm serious

This is my goodbye. I hope you will be okay

It started with a sudden crack

Slithering down my back

A gentle touch to my surprise

Was the beginning of my souls demise

Little did I know

I was the main character of your show

So taken by your sound

I couldn't tell I was breaking down

Piece by piece, within

Slowly my soul would begin

To break in all the cracked places

Revealing your many different faces

You left me mangling

Heart tangling

To twisted for even I to recognize

You had taken my soul as your prize

I'm still standing

Even I ask myself how

Time gives you understanding

I'm ready now

To love in a sensual way

No more sword fighting

I treasure each day

No more nail biting

The love inside of me

Smiles in the morning

I can now see

I'm no longer mourning

The fairytale

The happy ending

That's an old wise tale

I want a new beginning

I'm learning it's ok

To just Love

ME

Monday's

Can seem so mundane

But God woke me up today

So as I begin this day

I will keep my focus

Cast down any hocus pocus

Work hard towards my goals

Off my back adversity will roll

HAVE A BLESSED WEEK EVERYONE

Victory

Is rejecting societies

Ideology

Of the norm of humanity

And expressing your own identity

While seizing every opportunity

To your fullest ability

With integrity

And dignity

I'm trying to find my lost years

Is this God's plan or my midlife fears

I'm always told to hush don't make a noise

While on the inside I scream in rejoice

I want more than mediocrity

Why do I just receive the devils reciprocity

He wakes me up at 2 am to dance in my mind

Reminding me of those who left me behind

He joins me daily at coffee time

Telling me return to bed your sun will never shine

You'll never be of any worth

Go ahead, leave this earth

Not one soul will mourn for you

Your true friends are far and few

The devil and the mind can be the most barbaric team

I must detach them at their seam

As a child I watched you
Wanting to be you
Oh how I loved you
My heart raced for you
I thought you were the best you
I denied the real you
Telling officials they didn't know you
As an adult I damned you
When you left I couldn't mourn you
Revelation came today; I am you

Top half dropped, mid half spread

A lil gray on my head

Mismatched socks, flannel pjs

What do you mean I don't look the same these days

I know it's hard for you to see

The real beauty in me

When all you do is zip your pants and head to work

I even have to help you button your shirt

There's 28 hours in my day

Listen closely to what I'm about to say

What a women does you can't compare

A man would need to work 3 jobs to pay her daily fare

We tend to our needs last

 And take care of your needs fast

When you get that good woman hold her tight

Acknowledge her worth and treat her right

I kept holding my face

This memory I will never erase

You took me to a foreign place

Making sure you had an alibi for your case

I see why liquor needs a chase

I needed mace

To escape at a lions pace

I'm filled with disgrace

How did I arrive in this coroners space

God I need your grace

For this is a very dark place

Obituary read a fatal love case

You showed up at around 7 pm
Said I am taking you to the darkest place you've ever been
You see tonight will be like no other night
You think you know how to fight
I cant stop laughing
Gasping
Wait till you see what I have for you
You thought your troubles were behind you
You see I just went below your belt
Hit you in your heartfelt
And the best thing is you didn't even feel it
Your going to need a turnikit
I just got through firing 9 rounds
Metal into those holy sounds
All that rebuking you did of me
Ha, now where's your victory
I said I just shot your son 9 times
This is not just a rhyme
Did you hear what I said, your son is on deathbed

Sealy, are you ok?

You seem sad today

I smirked and kept walking

I could hear the other kids talking

I slid into my chair

Covered my eyes with my hair

Shoulders shrunk in

Come on Ms. Elmore please just begin

But of course not

I was going to be the lesson that was taught

Back to my desk she came

Sealy, she said as she knelt down, your just not the same

While turning away from her she gasped " who gave you
that black eye?"

I tried not to stutter in order to hold up my lie

I replied with fear, it it was my mom's hate

It's my fault, I make her so irate

I apologize, I didn't see you
I now know it was the wrong door I walked through
I had stayed in this dark room waiting for years
So many battles, so many tears
I called your name, no I screamed out to you
How could you have left me, how could you
So I began to sulk in pity each day
I let my soul waste away
Filled with bitterness, I became empty
When I looked in the mirror there was a ghost looking
back at me
Dark circles under my eyes
No longer water in my cries
Words without a voice
I danced to music playing Satan's noise
Left on a bridge awakened by rocks in my teeth
I had no vision only sounds of strangers saying she's not
breathing
Then your hand was over my heart
You leaned forward, telling me you carried me from the
start
It was Satan's room I had chosen to walk into and you
had been waiting patiently
Now is not your time, there still are great plans for me
I gasped and awoke with real tears
Gods love will keep me for the rest of my years

Why can't I have the normal life
The house , 2 kids , and be the special wife
No not me
My normal is a broken family
Always struggling to pay rent
Every Friday my boyfriend gets bent
Working graveyard as a custodian
Eviction notice taped on the door again
I keep following the yellow brick road
Before my faith begins to erode
I'm trying to break the generational curse
Before its my time to leave in a Hearse
Some days
I just want to runaway
To the middle of nowhere
Cut all my hair
Dye it Clairol #103
And start a brand new me
Wear all the clothes I'd never be caught dead in
Dance to the music singing about sin
New friends
Champagne and passionate love; my new life begins
The school bell rings, I must have drifted off at my job
Reality hits, back to my life of dreary hob knob

You planted roots inside my soul

To deep to pull

I fight the unification

Desperation

Labeled as crazy

Divided

Blind sided

Daily

No one can truly see

Only my better half knows

When the evil within me shows

It is the thorn

The porn

Of you and I within

Battling again

To be

Set free

I'm not going to leave just a footprint

I'm going to indent

Reinvent

Redefine

What comes to mind

When you say my name

One will claim

Oh what a dame

A smiling face

Full of grace

Dressed in kindness to her very end

She would have liked to be your friend

Is your heart as heavy as your hands
Your moods are like rubber bands
Up down then POP
Somber accusations below my belt, sometimes on top
Suddenly, without warning
Here comes the scorning
The reminders
Before I can grab my blinders
Oh the things I forgot to do
Forget all the hours I've stayed up with you
While you choked on life
Tip toeing around while you cut your coke with a knife
Daring me to walk out on you
If you only knew
I mentally left a LONG TIME ago
The real me you'll never know
Sadly your cure has not been found yet
My healing is waiting over the rainbow, safely kept
God has been watching all your sins
And your true side effects have yet to begin

Your one adjective away from victory

From obtaining everything you could ever see

Take that *t* off can't

Yell you CAN like it's a chant

It starts within

That's when you win

The battle within, that's the biggest war

When your feet hit the floor

You see it's all up to you

The you inside that says this I can do

Push yourself each day

Gods love will lead the rest of the way

Oh when I met your body was I enamored

It was your eyes I favored

I knew I wanted you to be mine

I wanted to freeze time

This had to be that real love stuff

I just couldn't get enough

Then I met your soul

The mole

In time

I felt I was doing time

What once was captivating

Now held me captive

Lying next to you

Was bondage too

Now my only thoughts of peace

Is knowing we all have in this world a date of release

Oh when I met your body was I enamored

It was your eyes I favored

I knew I wanted you to be mine

I wanted to freeze time

This had to be that real love stuff

I just couldn't get enough

Then I met your soul

The mole

In time

I felt I was doing time

What once was captivating

Now held me captive

Lying next to you

Was bondage too

Now my only thoughts of peace

Is knowing we all have in this world a date of release

I heard my birth was an accident
An uncelebrated event
Even I admit I was an odd looking baby
But how could nurturing have escaped me
From both my mom and my dad
That is beyond sad
The Drs labeled me as environmentally deprived
Was it in a tree that I arrived
I think psychology gets things twisted
Tosses big words around and we all are somewhere listed
It's just called love
I mean it's from above
It says it in the bible, we were not created to be alone
A rib from man, created a woman to have a happy home
Yet it seldom works that way
Men and women do not stay
Love leaves out the back door
With resentment all over the floor
Resentment and reminder describe me to a tee
The two reasons why it was so hard to love me

I truly believed I would die without you
My cardiac beats would be few
Then I would flat line
Without you by my side
Dried up and cold
Alone and old
At least on the inside
My love for you I could never hide
Late nights on the phone till dawn
So smitten with your air I felt guilty if I yawned
I saw a light around you
I thought people of your caliber were few
Then I met reality
It was another she
Everything opposite of me
She even had your name tattooed on her
And she had your daughter
To find your last name was really Lie
All our hellos were just her temporary goodbyes
Our twins are due in May
I wonder if she will be at your funeral today

I always dreamt of a life of royalty
Where finely everyone would respect me
No longer would I I be the black sheep of the family
The one they hid in the corner of the study
Taught.to be quiet amongst everyone
Never allowed outside to have fun
Ashamed of my irregularities
I believe they were merely intimidated
Simply fixated
On my ability
 To always smile through life's atrocities
Singing in the window as a little girl
Refusing to be swallowed by this cruel world
Clothes torn
Shoes worn
Freckles all over my body
Mamma swearing I'll never be anybody
I will I will you wait and see
Watch what happens to peculiar me
Someone will listen to my story
Someone will love me
Well I must go for now
My concert is over I must go out and take a bow

Careful when you meet her she knows just what to say

She pops up on any given day

Without notice

Sometimes with presents to give

She's only an acquaintance of mine

We've crossed paths a handful of times

We are on a first name basis

Our relations have not always been an oasis

I would be doing well, happy

And here she would come wanting all of me

If you think you don't know her, ask your mamma

I call her Kelly, last name Karma

Dear younger me

Step quietly into the unknown

Leave all fear at your broken home

You are different and that's okay

If someone hurts you, pause and pray

Remain true to your heart, but protect it

Because of it, great love it will beget

Display random acts of kindness

Avoid constant visitors bringing messiness

Do what is right, don't choose what is left

You will have a joyful life, I know, for we've already met

I sit pondering on my bathroom floor
A part of me wishing for more
That part is small
The demon part of me is so tall
My physical height is 5 feet 6 inches
The demon height is 6 feet 5 inches
So heavy and weary
My smiles are few, eyes always teary
Today feels strange
It's like the bathroom tile has been rearranged
Today the blinds were open and I could see
A sunlight shining through this ugly tree
Limbs broken, leaves brown
But on top was a nest of birds making a joyous sound
This mother tree had stayed rooted during the wind
So this new family could begin
Am I the root God? Aged, heavy and torn?
For everyone is gone and my heart is worn
I finally got up off the floor
Dried my tears and shut yesterday's door
I'm not real sure of how to take care of just me
Maybe with practice I will become that queen you see

Sweet Jesus in the name of love

Ask yourself am I good with God above

Are you smiling most of the time

Or making excuses for your behind

Pay attention to your intentions, don't be a clown

Love doesn't hit. PUT YOUR HANDS DOWN.

I yearn to be more

When my feet hit the floor

Let every step I take

Shatter past mistakes

Forget any negative thought

Replace old lies I have been taught

I might be 52

But my mind is brand new

My heart is even fuller

For in this family I am the ruler

I am more than the rock, I am the foundation

For the next 5 generations

I not only think I can I know I can

The house of little is where I began

Only with God have I came this far

It is he who put my dreams in my heart

I'm free
Free to be Me
Just popped the last string
From my internal being
Oh the pop hurt
I felt the blood squirt
I didn't know where my eyes would take me
To light or darkness, what would I see
Fourty years of loathe was all I had seen
A color of blue like my spleen
Sadness, defeat
Despair at my feet
Slowly tangled in lies
Looking in a mirror of despise
I slowly became tired of eating dirt
Of carrying the weight of hurt
Always buying rejections food
Always tolerating despairs mood
I decided to give hope a chance
I gave joy a glance
And slowly the strings cut
All the bondage that kept my soul put
Was lifting up when I called on prayer
And those strings of defeat are no longer there
I'm now free
Free to be Me

Stop in the name of love
Stop acting like there is no God above
Stop turning to violence
Your time will come for repentance
Then you will be bent over like the little lamb
Begging to be forgiven, I'm sorry master ,I am I am
All while breaking spirits with your petty words
When it's your spirit that's broke, get help, get heard
True strength does not strike a soul
It learns to respect their role
Lets start to like one another
Then soon we can love like sister and brothers
No one can defeat Mr. Time
Lets work with him, take that first step, try to be kind

Time can move so quickly when traveling with joy

Oh so slowly when moving with ploy

Why do we easily keep our head in the past

Yet complain how time moves so fast

You cant borrow, loan, or return time

Its as tricky as a rhyme

It gets away as soon as we appreciate it

Gives us at least one memory to never forget

Make time your best friend

Not who your chasing at the end

How dare you take life from me
When you came from me
You abuse me daily
I cannot get free
I am your mother
There is no other
This is the worst offense
I have no defense

Everything is
figureoutable.

i just want to fit
instead i sit
waiting for someone to want me
to see
my beauty
not just my ugly
i know i stand out
freckles
shackles
red hair
odor everwhere
mamma said, why bathe? you cant wash off the ugly?
so i'll just be
the ugly me
still waiting
anticipating
for that one
just one
to even just like me
everyone has left me
are you, the reader, even still here?
If so, are you a little off? a little queer?
different like me?
see what I see?
why cant i just fit in?
Love is so hard to get! it should be a sin
Ill just wait. I hope my maker does not reject me
that he was the one that created the ugly me

There's a leak
It's causing me to freak
Where is it coming from
Where had it begun
It's not from the toilet
Not the sink, I would know it
Everywhere I step it's wet
I can't tell the color yet
Wait.. it's burgundy
Hold on it's coming from within me
But where
Not my skin or hair
Nothing is hurting me
Could this be
My soul reminding me
It too needs to be free

I awoke to another day
With nothing to say
And everything to pray
Pray quietly they say
So your prayers will be okay
The devil won't hear what you say
I do believe the devil is in my way
At times all day
At other times he is away
How do we know it's a he I say?
Because it is so evil? Is that the right way?
She's are pretty evil too I must say
I'm more at comfort with it being he okay?
For how could a she cause so much pain in
one day
Leave bodies that lay
Children gone awray
Families destroyed in one day
Like a well masterminded play
But I awoke today
To pray
That our world find peace today

one by one
with a brick
I built a wall
around my heart
bricks chipped
with little white lies
sealed together with slaps
stacked 5 feet tall
by all the numbers in your phone
6 ft wide from all the times you left me alone
swearing to never love again
ugly old bricks
so no man would even glance at me
cement bricks to protect my heart
the top security system
and now I must live in a security system
while building my wall
you took my mind
i took revenge
i got life behind brick walls

I can never get over this fence
I've tried repentance
For the side I'm on
Is far too gone
My moral fence; I shouldn't even try
Always whistling failure sighs
Give up, go hide
Your not worthy of the other side
I've seen through the hole
A beautiful red haired soul
Smiling
Dancing
Wait that's me
A younger me
An actual beauty
Full of joy and integrity
This side is full of splinters made of should've
Built inside my mind of never could've

I never knew that you felt this way
Wow, okay
My hearts bouncing, I don't know what to say
Really, in a text your telling me this today
When did we get right here
I can't adhere
I can't adjust
An explanation is a must
Yet you won't reply
Text, calls, facebook, why
Here I am looking at a wedding cake
Yet you are planning my wake
Oh how tricky love can be
I savored your taste only for you to digest me

i just want to fit
instead i sit
waiting for someone to want me
to see
my beauty
not just my ugly
i know i stand out
freckles
shackles
red hair
odor everwhere
mamma said, why bathe? you cant wash off the ugly?
so i'll just be
the ugly me
still waiting
anticipating
for that one
just one
to even just like me
everyone has left me
are you, the reader, even still here?
If so, are you a little off? a little queer?
different like me?
see what I see?
why cant i just fit in?
Love is so hard to get! it should be a sin
Ill just wait. I hope my maker does not reject me
that he was the one that created the ugly me

I heard you

I heard you crying on the phone
Saying you were done
Tired of trying
Felt like dying
I wanted to stop you right then
Tell don't give up you can win
It's just a time it will go
But I didn't want to add to your low
So I just listened like most do
And turned my check and judged you
When I could've reached out my hand
And helped you from the quicksand
Too worried about me
I did not see
Your sincere pain
I used refrain
Justified my reason
Said oh it's just another season
She'll be fine
It's her mess not mine
Now your gone
I'm in a bigger mess of my own
Living in this circle of guilt and reprimand
Praying for someone to pull me from my quicksand

You left your mask
Picking it up was a task
I dropped it twice it was hot
Oh the pain it brought
From the heat; from the discovery
Of what was looking at me
The smirk irritated
My eyes fixated
This mask had been in my bed
Been in my head
For over a year
Reasons unclear
No texts not a goodbye
Not a tear not a why
You leave the only part of you
I ever knew

the most barbaric captor
of mankind
from beginning of time
still undefeated
                    is thy mind

So many elephants in my room where I used
to stay
But there were over 200 on any given day
200 people in this orphanage
Where I was held hostage
In the window I stayed
Never played
Bullied by the color of my hair
In that window, My anger kept me there
Staring at cars watching everyone drive
Chevys, Fords, and Pintos, Wishing one would
stop by
Rescue me rescue me please
I promise, I will put my mouth at at ease
For it was what got me here
I trusted a stranger and told my fear
I was then removed, separated
From my reality, segregated
Only twelve years old
I broke all every mold
Bad, ugly, unworthy, one of a kind
A child of a twisted mind
A frightened confession
Has Lead to my elephants expression

I hated me
And came to see
It is thy will
That I be still
And feel the pain
Of my vain
Thinking it was the others
My fellow brothers
Until I fell into the hole
Without a sole
Only my breath is all I heard
Out of breath, not a word
I had to see
It was all me
Left to bargain with only my shadow
Begging for another tomorrow
I realized
Why I am so despised
Mr.Time please help me repent
Before Hell I am to be sent.

Most often we say I forgive thee
Have you ever said I forgive me
Empty all your guilt out
Let that whisper be a shout
Told yourself yes you are number one
Your time has begun
No one can give you desire
It's like air in a tire
You have to put it in
You can it starts within
Faith the size of a mustard seed
And you will start to succeed
Please believe
That you are meant to conceive
The most beautiful message from above
That you were made to be filled with, live with
and grow from love.

when you pushed me out did you want
to push me back in
was I conceived out of sin
was your first vision of my face
a memory you've prayed to erase
was my first beating a true
consequence
or inner demons exuding dominance
I did not choose you as my mother
but I would never choose another
the loathe you spewed on my soul
taught me how to dance with ridicule
and yet I still wanted only your heart
a demons black breath kept us apart

do you see what I see? its giving me
quivers?
is that blood? no...it looks like chicken
livers!
all down my sleeve! on my left arm!
quick pull the fire alarm!
my sleeve is getting so very soaked!
I can't breathe I'm getting choked!
and suddenly I put my mind at ease
for I had forgotten to put my heart
back inside my sleeve!

that scar there
      he did not like my hair
the one on my knee
      he did not mean to
      throw me
this one on my chin
      I commited a sin
I spoke in public
      so I caught a yardstick
If his food is cold, I'll see anger
      I remove my clothes
      and catch a hanger
but his love is real love to me
      for this is exactly how
      mommy used to love me

Take back your Self Esteem
Go get your Dream
Peek in the Mirror
Do you see Her
That Striking Lady
Stop talking to Maybe
See your Queen
That Amazing Being
That can do Anything
LET GO of your old friend Doubt
Take a NEW ROUTE
LAUGH at your QUIRKS
REJECT the devil when it lerks
CLAIM YOUR VICTORY
YOUR BEAUTY IS YOUR ENTITY

So often I had to count on Penny

Penny always rescued me

My kids never met her

To them copper was a never

Or so they thought

If only they knew how things were bought

I often went to bed so hungry

Knowing Penny had somewhere else to be

Counting to the last Lincoln Memorial

Just to get the generic box of cereal

In the Walmart line late at night

Making sure I would be out of familiar sight

Oh God I only have $4.18

Yes God its only $4.17

Penny, my true friend

You have came to my rescue yet again

Hey Mr. Plans can we meet?
I'm not feeling so sweet
I had all these things I was to do
And yet the things crossed off are few
It seems you have been on an extended break
I tried calling you during my heartache
To book a road trip
That cruise on a ship
No reply or return call
How could you let me fall
Your my best friend. My Mr. Plans
Not just one I take on errands
From age 24 to 80 I had us all figured out
Success and happiness without a doubt
Yet you too took your own route
Leaving me too often cry and shout
Start all over in the middle
This feels like a riddle
Mr. Plans based on your past, its best to say
I will take you day to day.

Mankind

Can be so unkind

Blind

Playing footsy with ones mind

Rewind

Is Eve really to blame for the poisonous apple rind

Could you maybe dress me up in kindness today

I know, I know its daddy that makes you dance this way

You've brushed my hair with hate since I was three

Blaming my pregnancy on me

But you've had another child since

Let me guess, with her you were tied to a fence

I seem to be the cause of all your wrongs

The makings of a tortured love song

The only sad part

That's a twisted beat to a mothers heart

How on Earth could you?

Uneqivicabilly

Undeniably

Ungratefully

Untimely

Unremorsefully

Unexexplainingly

Eat the last spoonful of my Ben & Jerrys?

Love can be captivating

Never to be held captive

Two souls bound together

Never held in bondage

Lying side by side

Never a knife in ones side

Saying I do

Never your honor I didn't mean to

Always till death do we part

Never wanting DNR on ones heart

you bent and pulled , all while smiling
constantly filling my spirit with a foreign language
 no one but I would comprehend
to society I was disabled, a mute
for what my heart desired was freely given to the least common
but you made sure there was nothing common within me
 filled with maple venom
you would often stare waiting to make sure the sun
 never shined upon me
waiting with a cross in your hand
yet you were the first who lost the war when the death angel came
and I still sit longing for that free love
holding my own hand
listening to the rain as it beats like my pulse; thump, thump
visualizing what love truly wears
crisp white shirt, strong hands, desire cologne, slowly unwrapping my bondage
will I meet him before the death angel returns
and no one is mourning my love as I too am lowered next to you

Listening to your breaths melody
Not knowing the style it would turn to be
Love song, classic, or pure tragedy
Tears of mine joined in for the base
For this painful night I will never erase
First chorus your baby's been shot 7 times
I still look at the table for white dust lines
Violins keep playing as I pray
These beautiful minutes of time on replay
Death wanted to sing acapello
God refused, his voice is to mellow

You took my breath away
I was speechless
The first month was heaven
Now you can keep my air
I've learned a new language
Rents due in hell

A mighty wind roar
Police beating at the door
Fighting back tears
Rebuking fears
Turning left instead of right
Getting on the 12 hour flight
Raising two children alone
Paying for your parents home
Knowing you did your best
Laying a child to rest
Saying goodbye
Never knowing the why
Saying hello
Listening to bellow
Smiling through the pain
Dancing in the rain
Strong is a description, an act
A beautiful asset as a matter of fact

Hope cannot be seen or heard
Hope is a word
That helps one know
That this is not a show
That you will be okay
No your really going to be okay
For it is a new day
Things will not be the same way
Something around you has changed
Small things have been rearranged
Something is working for your good
You never thought it would

But way inside you
HOPE was waiting for its clue
You dont know the second it took place
When the pain was beginning to erase
When light was pushing through
When someone was praying for you
Finally. A knock. A feeling of cheer.
Hope is here.

A promise till death due us part
Usually made from from ones heart
Most common not to last
A fatal scar from the past
Spoken words meant to keep
Often led one to weep
How could one lie to another
Not stay forever
You promised
You are missed
I want your memory to fade
My mind and heart you still raid

The door

The door
What is it for
As youth we have no guard
No locks; ready for the yard
As teens anxiously await
The knock of that first date
As young adults the key to the new house
To the basement looking for that mouse
At middle age the break up, I'm moving out
Shut Slam Shout
As you age the phone call comes and you drop to the floor
Daddy is gone, the key to his door is needed no more
Life and all the doors in path
Often used to express ones wrath
Now 5 locks and a peephole
For this piece of wood protects the soul
The Door is often known to keep many apart
The Door most often closed is in thy heart

Can I place an order to go

I'm in a hurry you know

I need a new spirit

One without so much hurt in it

Can you add on joy

No, no I don't need a kids toy

I'm in a hurry, make it a super size of hope

Quick, I'm slipping down your drive thru slope

Pay God at the window

Pay with the seeds I've sewn

Well can I get an advance or a good deed to borrow

I understand I'll try back tomorrow

Finally, everything I've been waiting for

My prince to walk through the door

The prince of tides

Arms open wide

Here to rescue me

Ignoring my inequities

I jump into his arms

Never fearing harm

All my dreams have came to fruition

Without a petition

Then my receipt came

Glee did not feel the same

In fact it was dark and tight

As my casket lowered into forever nights

The good ole iron skillet
One can just smell it
The difference in the food
Puts you in the mood
To gather with family
Raise wine glasses with unity
When raised one often fled
For has been used against ones head
As resilient as a beautiful woman
Layer with mere olive oil; ready for the oven
Created in 1876 still holding strong
In everyone's kitchen one does belong

It was hard being the oldest seeing the things I saw
Everything around me was so raw
Dishes thrown
Stitches sewn
Electric always off
Missing school because of sisters cough
Mom always gone
Mismatched clothes on
Bullied at school
At home I made the rules
Caretaker, maid and black sheep
Food in my stomach I could never keep
To this day I'm still the odd ball
God is the only true one I can call
Family is sometimes just a word
But God, he heard
My many cries
He never denies
So you struggling keep your chin up
Gods Got You! Don't Give Up!

If only they knew

The things you really do

The names you call me

The bruises they do not see

The time you held me against my will

I felt I was chewing on a embalming pill

In public you smile

Walking smugly down each aisle

I cowardly push the cart

Avoiding all your darts

Anticipating the return home

My ISIS my danger zone

If only a friend, or even a stranger would take my cue

Then I could win the lottery and escape you

I've built up my strength, cast away cares

Obituary will read, accident fell down a flight of stairs

I smile

Feeling worthwhile

I focus

On us

Me and you Lord

My strong connecting cord

Wrapped around me always

Even tighter on rough days

A mighty presence you are

I know your never far

At times I took you for granted

Not worrying about the seeds I planted

If I fall to hard

I know I'm playing in the wrong yard

Thank you for always saving me

I look forward to our time in eternity

I am I am I am

All that I can be

Im not Im not Im not

That coward you see in me

I will I will I will

Rise each day

You wont you wont you wont

tear down my spirit today

I tried I tried I tried

To show you love

You pushed you pushed you pushed

I gave you to the Lord above

Im going Im going Im gone

To love me now

Goodbye , goodbye, so long

Our story is over, take a bow

Don't be pushing out your last air

Suddenly wanting to pay your fare

Constantly creating drama

Unfamiliar with karma

Walk in principle

Make giving habitual

Time; it can be contrary

What will be written in your obituary

ABUSE is a violation
An assignation
Of ones heart
Making one depart
From their very own
Comfort zone
No longer secure in their own skin
Questioning everything they've ever been
Knowing now all they will be
Is a human form of irregularity
Taking blame
Adopting shame
Hygiene said farewell
Any act of kindness only found in a wishing well
The second you decide to leave
Abuse rolls up his sleeve
Tells you come on stay awhile
No ones waiting on your smile

Oh no I didn't just send that text to him
For he will show it again
To this friend
That friend
This girl
That girl
I've ruined my entire world
Claiming my love, "Your my World"
I can't live without you
If you really leave me you know what I'll do
Come over and beg you
Scream to you
You know I'm the one
How could you be so dumb
To ever replace me
You took my virginity
I was only sixteen
It didn't feel so keen
But I loved you and went along
With your song
Romeo and Juliet
Now look, someone new you have met
No more me not even a goodbye lover
OMG I accidentally sent this to YOUR MOTHER

MOVE OVER MAKE ROOM

GOOD THINGS ARE COMING SOON

YOUR EGO IS IN THE WAY

THAT ATTITUDE CANNOT STAY

JOY WANTS TO FILL YOUR SPACE

SADNESS MUST BE ERASED

ANGER BEGETS ANGER

WHICH CAN LEAD ONE TO DANGER

JOY BEGETS JOY

HAPPINESS WILL COME WITHOUT A PLOY

You really thought you had broke me
and I would never rise to see
a better me
or what life could ever be
without thee
thy royalty
yet it is thee
that cannot see
the jewel in me
For I had already began to be
more than royalty
A child of thee most High Authority
Child of God you see
in your absence He took care of me
I'm not where you left me
only footprints of Him carrying me
sorry to disappoint thee

I just cant seem to let you go

The tighter I clinch the deeper you sew

Into the root of me

As if you dictate where I'll spend eternity

Is this love or lust

Enamor or disgust

When you breath I want to touch your air

Everyday I yearn to smell your hair

You inhale my soul

I've forgotten my role

Im no longer just one in my own skin

the connectors to your heart has no end

We all wear masks on a certain day

When consulted we confirm we are ok

Im just feeling under the weather

When deep down you know better

Your not just tired

You just got fired

Husband cheated

Cancer cant seem to be defeated

Your thoughts are racing

You cant stop pacing

Just enough food for the children

When will your trials ever end

Sit down and pray

No mess is here to stay

Gods got a plan for you

Hes working things out, your troubles will be few

Just hold on and smile

In the end it will all be worthwhile

Wearing the wrong size
To supersize
Your outside
Will only expose
What's decomposing
On the inside

Each time you knock me down
I pray I stay on the ground
I bargain with that little voice inside
Please just let me hide
I'll crawl into a hole
Just take me and my broken soul
I will leave the illusions
And contusions
Just erase my memory
From the time I was 23
When it all began
My face was held into the sand
Breath gone, death at my door
Now I'm 44
I'm tired ready to go
To a place where only strangers go
Pack my pain
Light him aflame
Even in a judicial cage
I am safe from his rage

There's a little lady in me that wants out

To turn on music and dance all about

Never being serious

Always curious

She only sees the good in all

No built up walls

For she still believes she can be a star

She never sees her scars

She's never been hit

In a corner she'll never sit

She wakes up with a smile on her face

No bad memories to erase

That little lady is now 52 year old

Battered, bruised and a heart of mold

What is depression
An impression
One in the mind
That one negative thought that binds
Sitting for hours in one spot
Replaying that the war you just fought
Questioning how important you really are
Trying and trying to deny you are bizarre
Hair tangled
Thoughts mangled
Memories a blur
Constantly wrapped in mammas fur
Pills or a shot
Whatever will kill that crazy thought
The mind and its friend
The one named Depression, can lead you to unlikely
end

Ladies we don't just work hard for our money
We work hard for ourselves, kids, and honeys
Entrepreneurs, moms and teachers
PTAs, tutoring, screaming in the bleachers
We're always told we think to much
Could a man handle all this amazing stuff
We have to lift our breasts
Wear the strong mom armor vest
Walk around in a girdle too small
4 inch heels, 1 wrong move and oh what a fall
We forget God pulled a rib from Adam
So when you men can't fathom
How we can do everything
God knew what he was creating

You left a film on me
Thick and binding
Black tar to be exactly
Ill be fine one minute then suddenly cannot see
Thoughts of you will linger in me
On and on for what seems like eternity
Feeling like the devil is inside of me
I try rebuking thee
Over and over repeatedly
Unsuccessfully
Until my mind and body are depleted of all sanity
I begin to cry. How could there be such cruelty
Why cant human beings just part amicably
End their stories and move on peacefully
Is the torment of the breakup more joyful to thee
Our dance in my mind has played such trickery
Piece by piece I must scrape away thoughts of thee
So I can begin to cleanse inside me

I gave you me

At the justice of the peace

You thought of me as broken

Your token

Always wearing a half smile

Reminding me I'm not worthwhile

Buying my clothes at the local thrift store

While you strut around wearing Dior

I began feeling this classy lady and practicing a walk

I would shut my mouth and listen to you talk

More and more curious of her and less of you

I suddenly knew what I had to do

Get away from you so she could be

For that classy lady was inside of me

I deserve to strut my Prada

Not second hand clothes of someone's mamma

My love to you was a gift

Take this ring and pawn it

My best friend Fatty protected me
From wrong love coming near me
All while surrounding the organs within me
It had to be a he that made me heavy enough to fight
 He kept me warm every night
In school I was teased, Fatty Patty they called me
I cried daily
So when people made fun of me
I turned to Fatty, for my beauty only he could see
Me and Fatty loved mac n cheese
But in the winter would he make me wheeze
The older I got the harder he was to carry
Drs said if I kept with him I'd die soon of a coronary
How was I to let Fatty go
He was my best friend you know
All we ever did was eat all day and talk
Then one day we started to take a walk
After three months Fatty made a confession to me
My best friend he could no longer be
He was moving on and so should I
This was our goodbye
That best friend of yours is really a she
GO! Look in your mirror and you will see what I see

Thank you for reading my writing.
These were composed as I journeyed
through life stages.
Orphaned, sexual abuse, adoption,
epilepsy, cancer death,
family shooting, entire family having covid-19,
mental health issues, domestic abuse,
MS disease
and heart disease.
And I can say I am still standing.
Walking in this journey called life.
I am no longer running from trials of my past.
I can now say I live in today,
in the joy of being a woman warrior.

Shannon Patty